Zen For Beginners

A Beginners Guide to Zen

Introduction

I would like to thank you for downloading the book, *"Zen For Beginners - A Beginner's Guide To Zen"*.

In saying, *"Peace comes from within. Do not seek it without,"* Buddha is 100 percent right. Even if you possess all the luxuries wealth can buy, you cannot be happy and excited about your life if you are not peaceful from the inside.

How can you learn to cultivate inner peace and a sense of fulfillment while the world we live in is as a fast-paced and stressful one where because we have so many responsibilities to attend and so much work to do, it often becomes nearly impossible to be peaceful and happy?

While it is true that we live in a hectic and stressing world, this does not mean you can never attain inner peace and fulfillment. You can certainly be peaceful and fulfilled even as you fulfill your responsibilities and enjoy your life. How can you do that? Well, the answer is simple: *Zen*

Zen is a branch of Buddhism that focuses mainly on meditation and teaches you ways to infuse peace and calm into your routine life. If you desire to learn all about Zen and follow Zen practices, this book is for you.

Created as a complete Zen guide for beginners, this book illuminates Zen and its benefits along with easy-to-follow steps guaranteed to help you bring the essence of Zen into your everyday life and thus make your life more meaningful, peaceful, and harmonious.

Thanks again for downloading this book, I hope you enjoy it!

The trademarks that are used are without any consent, and the publication of the trademark is without permission or backing by the trademark owner. All trademarks and brands within this book are for clarifying purposes only and are the owned by the owners themselves, not affiliated with this document.

Table of Contents

A Closer Look At Zen

Zen is a branch of Buddhism that focuses on meditation. Although Zen centers on meditation and uses that practice to help you live a tranquil, serene life, the truth is that Zen is an impossibly difficult concept to describe using mere words. Zen is a way of life and your grasp of it depends entirely on your intuition. Bodhidharma, one of the legendary Buddhist monks who spread Chan Buddhism in China once described Zen in the following words,

"Not dependent on the written word,

Transmission apart from the scriptures;

Directly pointing at one's heart,

Seeing one's nature, becoming Buddha"

If you observe this poem closely, you will understand that the essence of Zen lies in knowing yourself completely. Zen is an attitude you adopt once you understand who you are and why you are as you are in this moment. Zen is about knowing your heart and seeing your nature so you can understand your true self because only then can you attain inner peace just as Buddha did.

When you know yourself completely and live in the moment, you start to distance yourself from everything that does not matter to you; you instead focus solely on improving your life by doing meaningful things.

Buddha attained nirvana, the state of eternal peace and bliss by understanding himself. He went into a meditative state for a long time. During this time, he understood the four noble truths of life, which is how he ended up better understanding himself and the human nature.

Why do we mention Buddha and the four noble truths here? Well, we do so because Zen is a branch of Buddhism based on the four noble truths. Buddhism centers on the fundamentals of the *truths* and the *eightfold path* that both elaborate how to attain a state of inner peace.

Hence, to understand Zen, you need to understand these two.

The Four Noble Truths

Zen centers on the 'four noble truths' that describe why we experience sufferings in the world.' The four noble truths are as follows:

1: The Noble Truth of Dukkha: This is the first noble truth. It states that there exists suffering in the world, suffering broadly categorized into mental, emotional, and physical suffering.

All of us experience any one of these or even all these sufferings at the same time. Either we feel mentally hurt or upset by something undesirable in our lives, or we experience physical suffering; either way, we hurt and feel miserable.

This truth gives insight into the fact that suffering is always present in the world and suffering is something none can fully escape. However, we can lessen suffering and make it less important. To do that, the first thing is to acknowledge this truth.

2: The Noble Truth of the Origin of Dukkha (Truth of Reason Behind Suffering): The second truth points out exactly why we suffer. We suffer because we never stop desiring things. We demand things all the time. Whether it is a big house, love of your life, smarter kids, or a good job, our desires never end. When we fail to fulfill our desire, we welcome suffering into our lives.

3: The Noble Truth of the Cessation of Dukkha (Truth Culmination of Dukkha): The third noble truth, the culmination of Dukkha, offers an antidote to our sufferings: ***stop desiring things.***

When you stop desiring for more and better, you stop suffering because you detach meaning, happiness, and value to things. That does not mean you stop loving people or stop enjoying life, it just means you let go of all attachments you have with the things you feel are essential for you.

4: The Noble Truth of the Path Leading to the Cessation of Dukkha (Truth of the Middle Path): This is the fourth truth. It provides a way to ease all your sufferings for good.

Known as the middle way, to live a brilliant, happy life, this path requires you to follow eight rules and to detach yourself from all the sufferings. This path is exactly what Zen is about and precisely the thing meditation can help you achieve.

We will first describe this path, aka Eightfold Noble Path, and then describe its role in Zen.

The Eightfold Noble Path

The eightfold noble path describes eight rules you need to follow to cleanse your heart, soul, and body of all sorts of desires and malpractices so you can attain inner peace. These eight rules are usually categorized into three divisions: *wisdom that comprises of the first two guidelines, ethical conduct that encompasses the third, fourth, and fifth rules*, and *concentration that comprises of the last three rules*. Here are those eight rules:

1: Samma Ditthi: Known as 'right view' in English, samma ditthi means to improve your view and perception of things so you can find the truth about things. Often, we perceive things as presented to us without questioning the validity of that view. This often causes us to trust and accept incomplete and wrong information.

For instance, if you see a man in old rags, smoking a cigarette, and mischievously looking at you, you may think of him as a thief or a homeless person.

What if that person owns a mansion and owns many charitable organizations? You can never guess that just by looking at him, right, but since that is the information immediately available to you, you use that to form your judgment of that man.

By following samma ditthi, you learn to correct your perception of things and stop judging people and things unless you have all the information you need to come to a logical and reasonable conclusion.

2: Samma Sankappa: Samma sankappa is the Sanskrit term used for the 'right intention.' This essentially means to have the right intentions for everyone. You must never think evil of, or for anyone, and to become full of hope, positivity, and happiness, you must hold compassion for humanity.

3: Samma Vacca: Samma vacca or 'right speech' means to give up backbiting, slanderous talk, gossiping, and negative self-talk. You have to talk positively to yourself and to others so you can set the right intentions for everyone and improve your view of the world around you.

4: Samma Kammanta: Samma kammanta loosely translates to the 'right action' in English and means to improve your actions and behaviors. You can do this by shunning all types of wrongdoings such as sexual misconduct, illegitimate behaviors, and doing things that harm and hurt others.

5: Samma Ajiva: Samma ajiva or 'right livelihood' means to desist from engaging in illegal means of earning a living; this includes dealing in poisonous substances, intoxicants, flesh, weapons, and prostitution.

6: Samma Vayama: Samma vayama is Sanskrit for 'right effort' and means to channelize your effort and energies to all things right, healthy, and positive. Your effort becomes right when you pay heed to the first five rules.

7: Samma Satti: Samma satti or 'right mindfulness' means to be, and dwell in the state of mindfulness. Mindfulness means to be fully aware of your life and each moment as it passes without being judgmental of it and without attaching any negative meaning to things. Only when you are mindful can you perceive things as they are and become fully conscious of yourself.

8: Samma Samadhi: 'Right concentration' or samma Samadhi in Sanskrit is the last rule of the eightfold noble path. It means to improve your state of concentration and focus completely on one thing at a time.

The reason why we perceive things the wrong way, have wrong intentions, or indulge in wrong practices closely relates to how we focus on things. Often, we do not focus fully on the thing we are doing, saying, or listening. This makes us perceive it the wrong way.

This also makes us half involved in activities we do, which makes us disregard their importance. This not only sucks happiness and joy out of those activities, it also increases our routine stress. By learning to concentrate better, we start to understand things better and become more interested in life as a whole, which obviously improves our quality of life.

By following these eight guidelines, you can make way for a happier, more fulfilled, and empowered life. But, where does Zen fit into this equation? How does it help you implement these rules and end your sufferings? Here is how.

How Zen Ends Suffering

Zen ends suffering by helping you understand yourself through meditation. Only when you know yourself can you find what is wrong with your life and why it is wrong. When you know your true self and how it makes your life tough, miserable, and complicated, you can then begin the work of improving yourself by following the right guidelines to live a balanced, amazing life.

Everything starts with knowing yourself better. A quote in Thich Nhat Hanh's book **Zen Keys** nicely sums up what Zen is and how it ends your problems.

The quotes states, *"One obvious answer is – through Zen. Not necessarily Zen Buddhism, but Zen in its broad sense of a one-pointed aware mind; of a disciplined life of simplicity and naturalness as against a contrived and artificial one; of a life compassionately concerned with our own and the world's welfare and not self-centered and aggressive. A life, in short, of harmony with the natural order of things and not in constant conflict with it."*

By following Zen and incorporating it into your life, you unleash your true, positive self, and live a life governed by eternal bliss, compassion, and peace because you stop doing meaningless things and stop attaching importance to materialistic possessions.

Now that you know what Zen is, let us get started with how you can bring it into your life.

Step 1: Simplify Your Life And Focus Only On The Essentials

To live a more meaningful life and distance yourself from sufferings, get down to the basics and get rid of the extra clutter in your life. The reason why you focus so much on plenty of things and feel unhappy and chaotic is that your life is full of clutter.

Too many ideas in your mind, things in your house, clothes in your wardrobe, and activities in your routine are the clutter we are talking about.

Centering your life on what matters, knowing your priorities, and the things that truly make you happy requires you to discern between the important and unimportant things in your life. Here is how you can simplify your life.

1: Cleanse Your Mind

To focus on things that really matter to you and to understand exactly what adds value to your life, you need to cleanse your mind of unnecessary and negative thoughts, ideas, and beliefs.

You pollute your mind with meaningless and unhealthy thoughts and ideas because of the type of mental food you feed your mind. Mental food refers to the ideas and thoughts you inject into your mind by reading and watching different things and spending time with various people.

If you spend time with influential, positive, and happy people, read healthy material, and watch videos and movies that focus on adding happiness and peace into your life, you will naturally think in a more positive direction.

As opposed to this, if you hang around the wrong kind of people who introduce you to heinous practices and professions, or those who make you negative and never inspire you to be better, and if you waste time watching, reading, and listening to things that lure you towards unhealthy practices, naturally, you will think that way too.

While meditation will help you cleanse your mind, as stated earlier, Zen is a way of life: a lifestyle composed of everything you do. To purify your mind of thoughts that bring you displeasure and stress, you need to feed on the right mental food. To do that, do the following:

Know exactly what brings you happiness: Do you spend time with friends who bring you down, or with someone who inspires you to live a simpler, more focused, and positive life? Do you feel more peaceful when watching porn or when you listen to an inspirational lecture on being compassionate to people?

Explore these and similar questions and write down these answers in a journal. You will be amazed at what you write down and will be surprised at how you never knew you had a more positive and compassionate side.

Understand the type of mental food you really need: Once you have a better understanding of what makes you feel good, think of the people you spend time with, the things you watch, and those you read. Find out which of those elements make you feel happy and good.

Get rid of the wrong sort of mental food: Eliminate from your life all the people and practices that unleash your negative and unhealthy side. If hanging out with a friend tempts you to indulge in illicit activities like fornication, something that makes you feel bad later on, stop hanging out with that friend.

Do not take his/her calls or visit places that he/she hangs out. Alternatively, you can firmly inform that friend of your intention to detach from him/her. Soon, he/she will get the message and stop bothering you.

If you spend hours watching movies online, something that does not add value to your life, block those sites and instead watch videos, and listen to lectures that help you find your purpose in life.

Doing all of this takes courage and time; be patient with yourself, and slowly infuse these practices into your daily life. You do not have to give up everything right now; taking baby steps each day is the best approach. Maintaining a journal and writing daily notes of how you bring little changes into your life is a great way to become more involved in the process, acknowledge your little and big accomplishments, and be proud of yourself.

After adding the right mental food to your life, cleanse your life of the unwanted materialistic clutter.

2: Get Rid of Materialistic Clutter

As you cleanse your mind, you will get rid of many unhealthy thoughts that cause you to stockpile materialistic things and that create heaps of physical clutter in your house and workplace.

Heaps of clothes you have not worn for years and do not plan to wear in the coming years, big and small pieces of furniture passed on to you but those that hardly mean anything to you, and all the meaningless utensils, ornaments, decorative pieces, wall art, etc. fall in the category of materialistic category.

This category essentially encompasses things you do not use often, items that are not important to you and those that are just adding to the routine clutter in your house.

Physical clutter often results in mental clutter because when you have so many things to care for, you naturally experience stress. Moreover, the huge variety of stuff packed in your house often distracts you from meaningful tasks and ideas, and makes you focus on things that do not really matter.

For instance, you may have a plan to become a philanthropist but your habit of hoarding stuff has caused you to forget that goal you once set and has instead made you a victim of your own desires. When your desires enter the equation, suffering steps in too.

Even without your realization, you incapacitate yourself mentally and physically. Thus, this means to let go of desires and sufferings, and to become a Zen practitioner, you have to let go of the clutter in your life. To do that, examine your house and workplace in detail and create a list of all items that no longer hold meaning for you but in turn increase your unnecessary desires.

Once you identify such things, slowly get rid of them by donating them to charitable organizations, giving them to friends and family who could put them to better use, and discard items in bad condition.

Remain only with that which you truly need, want, and like. After de-cluttering your life and keeping the meaningful stuff, pen down your feelings. How peaceful, happy, and serene you feel shall amaze you. As you make these changes an integral part of your life, you will start to explore and understand yourself better, and will begin to comprehend the meaning of Zen.

To further improve this understanding and live the true Zen life, you also need to improve your actions. To do that, you have to re-evaluate your aspirations, goals, and ambitions. In the next step, we shall be discussing this very aspect.

Step 2: Improve Your Actions By Re-Assessing Your Goals And Aspirations

One popular Zen saying states, *"It is the silence between the notes that makes the music; it is the space between the bars that cages the tiger."* Adding to this quote, what we do daily and our goals make up our lives.

We are all striving to achieve something. This something could be more wealth, better health, increased happiness, or improved relationships: the fact remains each of us has some sort of aim we are somehow trying to achieve. This struggle to accomplish our goals is what creates our overall life experiences.

To live a Zen life, it is essential that we focus on improving this aspect of our experience of life so we live a high quality life. Here is how you can work on improving your goals and dreams.

Improve Your Goals And Dreams

Improving your life goals, ambitions, and dreams means you have to reevaluate your current goals and set ones that really matter to you. We often set goals we feel can add value to our lives and can make us truly happy.

However, and as is often the case, we end up quitting those goals and jumping to new ones because the first set of goals did not matter much to us. This shifting from one goal to another often brings us nothing but undue stress.

Moreover, when we find a goal we feel strongly connected to, we tend to build so much attachment to it that we feel our life will not feel fulfilled unless we accomplish that goal. We strive hard to fulfill that goal only to find that contentment was not relative to that accomplishment.

To feel content and happy, we set another goal again and repeat the cycle all over again. This cycle continues and we never truly attain the fulfillment we want.

To bring satisfaction and peace in our lives, we MUST reevaluate all our goals and develop the right sort of attachment to them.

How To Re-Assess Your Goals And Dreams

While you should strive to achieve your goals and dreams, it should not be to the extent that the pursuit of their fulfillment brings you stress and anxiety. Here is how you can do that.

1. Think of all your current goals, dreams, and ambitions and write them down in your journal.

2. Think of why you want to accomplish them. Is it because you feel they will help you become happy or wealthy, or because you feel as if your entire life revolves around them?

On a scale from 1 to 10, rate how you feel about your goal with 1 being the lowest and 10 being the highest. If you strongly feel about your goal and pursuing it is not stressful for you, this goal is a meaningful one.

3. Identify any ideas and thoughts connected to your goals and dreams. By this, we mean thoughts such as "I can only be happy if I achieve a certain goal," or "If I don't achieve this (name of goal), I can never be fully satisfied."

Identifying such thoughts may take a little time; give yourself a few days so you can be truly sure of how you feel about your goal. Once you identify those harmful thought patterns, eliminate them by setting more peaceful and meaningful goals.

4. Evaluate your goal based on the description of 'right livelihood.' Does your goal cause you to hurt others? Does your goal relate to something illegitimate? Think of the different actions you have to take daily to fulfill your goal. Are they illegal or destructive? If they in anyway pose threat and inflict harm on someone, they are illegitimate and will bring you and he humankind in general stress. You therefore should disregard such goals.

5. To set meaningful goals that infuse peace into your life, think of a goal that comprises of the right action, right intention, and right livelihood as described in the eightfold noble path. For instance, if you have a knack for writing and earlier used to write on erotica, you could now use your skill to write self-development books that help people live a better life.

6. Once you reevaluate your goals and ambitions and set a new goal that holds more meaning to you, write it down. Take a few minutes to think about it and visualize it. If you notice that you feel peaceful, as you think of that goal, that is the perfect aim for you. If not, keep searching for a more meaningful and suitable goal.

7. The next thing is to think of all the different things you should do on a daily basis to achieve your goal. This helps you simplify your routine and daily actions so you work in the right direction every day and live a Zen life every day of the rest of your life. If for instance, your goal is to help people live a better life, do something kind for those around you every day.

While you should strongly feel passionate about your goal, make sure your attachment to it stays moderate. As stated before, Zen teaches you to adopt the middle way in everything, which is why we call the eightfold path the middle path. This ensures you never become involved in the materialistic world and do not freak out while pursuing your goals.

To ensure you stay on the right track for good, you need to stay fully conscious of your thoughts and emotions. This helps ensure you do not overly attach yourself to the wrong things, which helps you live a well-balanced life. This is where meditation comes in handy. Move ahead to the next step where you shall discover how to practice Zen meditation.

Step 3: Meditate To Be More Aware Of Yourself

Mario Quintana, a Brazilian writer and translator better known as the poet of "simple things" once said, *"Don't wait for someone to bring you flowers. Plant your own garden and decorate your own soul."*

If you wait for people to bring you happiness, you will never find true satisfaction. To live a happy, content life, you have to exert the effort needed to incorporate happiness into your life: *You should create your own garden and invest time and effort into cleansing and beautifying your soul.*

This is what Zen meditation is all about.

The reason you had to simplify your life and reassess your goals prior to discussing meditation is that meditation requires you to still your mind and focus on one thing at a time. When you have a lot going on in your life, focusing on one particular thought or object does not come easy.

On the other hand, when your life is simple and your goals align with what your soul desires, concentrating on important things such as your breath or an important thought comes naturally.

Now that you have simplified your life, it is time to add meditation into your life. Here is how you can practice it.

How To Practice Zazen

Zazen means seated meditation, which is the fundamental element of Zen. Zazen helps you gain a better understanding of yourself and as you start knowing who you are, you start detaching yourself from the meaningless things in life. This further helps you simplify your life and purify your heart, soul and body. Here is how you can practice Zazen.

Step 1 – Find a peaceful, meditation spot and a zafu: To meditate properly, find a peaceful spot free from distractions so you can fully focus on the practice at hand. Meditate anywhere quiet and peaceful, and try to reserve that area for meditation only so your mind associates the place with meditation.

You could place ornaments and objects that make you feel peaceful in that spot and take out all sorts of distractions such as a television. Once you find and settle into that spot, get a Zafu, which is a round, soft pillow designed specifically for meditating. It raises you off the ground so your back does not slouch and you do not sink into the ground. This keeps you upright and solely focused on the practice.

While it is best to practice Zazen while sitting on a Zafu, a Zafu is not compulsory. You can meditate sited on the ground, on a chair, or even on a couch. Zen is not about restricting you and making you uncomfortable. If you therefore find it easier to meditate while sitting on a chair, by all means do it.

Once you become more stable in the practice and can maintain your balance on a Zafu, get one and meditate using it. Whenever you meditate, wear loose, comfortable clothes so you can feel relaxed and do not keep tugging at your pants during the practice.

Step 2 – Choose a time to meditate: Next, pick a time to meditate. Choose any time you will be mostly free and will not feel the urge to do something else as you meditate. Also, pick an amount of time you can easily use for nothing but meditation. For starters, it is best to stick to a 2 minute meditation session so it does not feel challenging.

Moreover, stick to the meditation time you pick because doing so cultivates consistency and punctuality. If you meditate at 8am twice for 5 minutes, meditate for 5 minutes daily at 8 in the morning and increase your meditation duration only when you can easily stick to the longer time period.

Step 3 – Choose a Pose: To practice Zazen, experts recommend you adopt any one of the following meditative poses. Choose one pose you find most comfortable; if you do not feel comfortable in any of these poses yet, sit in whichever pose you find comfortable and you can select any one of these poses as your flexibility and balance improve.

Half Lotus

In the Hankafuza or half lotus pose, you place your right foot on your left thigh or left foot on the right thigh. You then gently tuck the other leg beneath the opposite leg.

Full Lotus

In the Kekafuza or full lotus pose, you place each foot on the opposite thigh. This pose is usually challenging for beginners, which is why most beginners opt to use the half lotus and slowly shift to the full lotus.

Burmese Pose

In this pose, you cross both your legs and your knees should lie on the ground. Ensure your ankles do not lie over each other.

Seiza Pose

This is a very simple pose wherein you kneel completely on the floor and keep your hips rested on your ankles.

Step 4 – Bring Your Awareness to Your Breath: Once you are in your meditation spot and are ready to meditate, think of anything calming, and then close your eyes. Slowly bring your attention to your breath and stay with it. As you inhale, say, *"I am with my in-breath"* and as you exhale, say, *"I am with my out-breath."*

Keep doing this and if your mind wanders off in thought, count your breath. This practice will slowly bring your attention back to your breath.

When your meditation period ends, gently open your eyes and slowly bring your awareness back to the real world. You will feel a lot more peaceful than before. Slowly increase your meditation duration to 5, 10, 20, 30, 45, and 60 minutes.

As you become better at, and more focused in the practice, start contemplating the different thoughts as they enter your mind. Instead of silencing your thoughts, let them enter and leave your mind and explore them as they emerge. This slowly helps you understand your thought pattern and then distance yourself from thoughts that birth desires and in turn your sufferings.

To free yourself from unnecessary desires and the suffering that accompanies them, try shunning dualistic thinking and adopt a non-dualistic approach.

Step 5 – Shun Dualistic Thinking: Throughout the course of your life, you have learnt there are good and bad things, there is wrong and right, healthy and unhealthy, and so on. This way of thinking is misleading because it postulates that if bad did not exist in the world, there would be no good; that if it were not for all your struggles and challenges, you would not have the ability to acknowledge your accomplishments and happiness.

The hardships, obstacles, and undesirable things you experience in life should be appreciated and accepted because they give you the opportunity to experience all the joy, beauty, and peace, your life has to offer.

The dualistic thinking we nurture makes us separate things from each other and forces us to perceive some things as good and others as bad. This is why certain things bother us so much. To stop perceiving things the wrong way, and to explore the essence of things, let go of dualistic thinking. Meditation helps with this task.

As you become better at meditating, adopt a non-judgmental attitude towards your life, different experiences, and every thought you experience. Instead of labeling a thought as negative or positive, explore it for what it is. This helps you establish new and unbiased relationships with different occurrences so they stop affecting you the way they once did.

For example, if you previously thought of betrayal as a sin but after shunning dualistic thinking, you may now believe that people change and so do their priorities. This new thinking helps you stay calm and patient even when someone betrays you because you no longer perceive betrayal as something hurtful.

Conclusion

Thank you again for downloading this book!

Lao Tzu said, *"The journey of a thousand miles must begin with a single step"* and boy was he right.

To accomplish something, you must begin with a single step. Similarly, to live a Zen life, you have to take action. Put the knowledge we have discussed in this book to good use and use it to improve your life.

Finally, if you enjoyed this book, would you be kind enough to leave a review for this book on Amazon?

Click here to leave a review for this book on Amazon!

Thank you and good luck!

Lightning Source UK Ltd.
Milton Keynes UK
UKHW022017250220
359329UK00008B/57

9 780648 011811